Mediterranean Refresh Cooking for Two

500-Day Perfectly Portioned Recipes for Healthy Eating

that Busy and Novice Can Cook on Budget

Podry Jamos

© Copyright 2021 Podry Jamos - All Rights Reserved.

In no way is it legal to reproduce, duplicate, or transmit any part of this document by either electronic means or in printed format. Recording of this publication is strictly prohibited, and any storage of this material is not allowed unless with written permission from the publisher. All rights reserved.

The information provided herein is stated to be truthful and consistent, in that any liability, regarding inattention or otherwise, by any usage or abuse of any policies, processes, or directions contained within is the solitary and complete responsibility of the recipient reader. Under no circumstances will any legal liability or blame be held against the publisher for any reparation, damages, or monetary loss due to the information herein, either directly or indirectly.

Respective authors own all copyrights not held by the publisher.

Legal Notice:

This book is copyright protected. This is only for personal use. You cannot amend, distribute, sell, use, quote or paraphrase any part of the content within this book without the consent of the author or copyright owner. Legal action will be pursued if this is breached.

Disclaimer Notice:

Please note the information contained within this document is for educational and entertainment purposes only. Every attempt has been made to provide accurate, up-to-date and reliable, complete information. No warranties of any kind are expressed or implied. Readers acknowledge that the author is not engaging in the rendering of legal, financial, medical or professional advice.

By reading this document, the reader agrees that under no circumstances are we responsible for any losses, direct or indirect, which are incurred as a result of the use of information contained within this document, including, but not limited to, errors, omissions, or inaccuracies.

Table of contents

Introduction 5
Chapter 1: Overview 6
    What is the Mediterranean diet? 6
    The history of the Mediterranean diet? 6
    The Science Behind Mediterranean diet 7
    Benefits of the Mediterranean diet 7
Chapter 2: Breakfast & Brunch 9
    Date Apple Oats 9
    Healthy Cauliflower Mushroom Salad 10
    Pepper Chickpea Salad 11
    Quinoa Breakfast Bowls 12
    Breakfast Rice Bowls 13
    Spinach Egg Breakfast 14
    Simple Breakfast Quinoa 15
    Simple Lemon Quinoa 16
Chapter 3: Soups & Stews 17
    Chicken Rice Soup 17
    Easy & Delicious Beef Stew 18
    Creamy Chicken Soup 19
    Simple Black Bean Soup 20
    Celery Soup 21
    Nutritious Kidney Bean Soup 22
    Pepper Pumpkin Soup 23
    Creamy Squash Cauliflower Soup 24
Chapter 4: Pasta, Grains & Beans 25
    Garlic Onion Pinto Beans 25
    Mac & Cheese 26
    Delicious Pasta Primavera 27
    Pesto Chicken Pasta 28
    Corn Risotto 29
    Chicken Risotto 30
    Delicious Chicken Pasta 31
    Creamy & Tasty Risotto 32
Chapter 5: Vegetables 33
    Italian Tomato Mushrooms 33
    Delicious Cauliflower Rice 34
    Healthy Vegetable Medley 35
    Healthy Chickpea & Broccoli 36
    Creamy Lemon Bell Peppers 37
    Creamy Dill Potatoes 38
    Potato Salad 39
    Radish & Asparagus 40
Chapter 6: Appetizers 41
    Spicy Jalapeno Spinach Artichoke Dip 41
    Olive Eggplant Spread 42
    Pinto Bean Dip 43
    Homemade Salsa 44
    Flavorful Roasted Baby Potatoes 45
    Healthy Kidney Bean Dip 46
    Balsamic Bell Pepper Salsa 47
    Kidney Bean Spread 48
Chapter 7: Poultry 49

Perfect Chicken & Rice 49
Moroccan Chicken 50
Tasty Turkey Chili 51
Flavorful Cafe Rio Chicken................. 52
Pesto Chicken 53
One Pot Chicken & Potatoes............. 54
Delicious Gyro Chicken 55
Flavorful Mediterranean Chicken 56

Chapter 8: Beef 57
Tasty Beef Stew 57
Italian Beef Roast 58
Beef Curry.. 59
Jalapeno Beef Chili 60
Italian Beef... 61
Cauliflower Tomato Beef 62
Lemon Basil Beef 63
Sage Tomato Beef 64

Chapter 9: Pork... 65
Lime Salsa Pork Chops 65
Basil Pork Broccoli............................... 66
Delicious Pork Roast............................ 67
Simple Paprika Pork Chops................ 68
Simple Lemon Pepper Pork Chops.... 69
Garlic Parsley Pork Chops.................. 70
Pork with Carrots Potatoes 71
Tasty Pork Carnitas 72

Chapter 10: Lamb 73
Delicious Salsa Lamb 73
Flavors Lamb Ribs................................ 74
Herb Veggie Lamb 75
Garlic Mushrooms Lamb Chops 76
Tasty Lamb Leg 77
Healthy Lamb & Couscous 78
Curried Lamb Stew.............................. 79
Lamb with Beans 80

Chapter 11: Seafood & Fish 81
Shrimp Scampi..................................... 81
Basil Fish Curry 82
Crab Stew.. 83
Quick & Easy Shrimp.......................... 84
Dijon Fish Fillets 85
Delicious Lemon Butter Cod 86
Lemoney Prawns.................................. 87
Lemon Cod Peas.................................. 88

Chapter 12: Desserts 89
Delicious Apple Pear Cobbler 89
Applesauce 90
Lime Pears... 91
Sweet Pear Stew................................... 92
Vanilla Apple Compote....................... 93
Blackberry Jam 94
Chocolate Nut Spread 95
Cinnamon Apple Rice Pudding......... 96

Conclusion 97

Introduction

The Mediterranean Refresh Cooking for Two will open your eyes to living a healthy lifestyle with perfect meals for two that take half an hour or less to prepare. Bring home the taste of the Mediterranean Refresh with these fantastic and delicious recipes. You will finally be able to prepare better and tastier meals in no time for you, your family, and friends.

This guide is particularly suitable for people without much experience in cooking Mediterranean Refresh cuisine as it includes all the information you need to get started, while further catering to the varied learning styles of different people.

With crisp veggies, succulent seafood, hearty grains, and healthy oils, the Mediterranean Refresh diet makes nutritious eating a pleasure. This cookbook brings its bright flavors and bountiful health benefits to your table with recipes designed for two people. No need to fuss over recipe conversions or deal with too many leftovers—just relax and savor a breezy seaside breakfast or a simple rustic dinner, all without leaving home.

Chapter 1: Overview

Mediterranean diet is not just a diet plan it is one of the healthy eating lifestyles. Most of the scientific study and research conducted over the Mediterranean diet proves that the Mediterranean diet helps to reduce your excess weight, cancer cell reduction and also reduces the risk of cardiovascular diseases.

Most of the scientific study also proves that the food consumption during the Mediterranean diet like vegetables, whole grain, nuts, fish and seasonable fruits improves blood vessels functions and reduce the risk of metabolic syndrome.

What is the Mediterranean diet?

Mediterranean diet is one of the traditional diets comes from different Mediterranean countries and regions. Mediterranean diet is basically a plant-based diet that allows you high consumption of vegetables, fruits, nuts, beans, grains, fish and olive oil. Mediterranean diet is a rich fat diet, it allows near about 40 percent of calories from fat. It also allows for consuming a moderate amount of protein and low consumption of meat and dairy products.

Mediterranean diet linked with good health and a healthier heart, it helps to reduce your health issues like diabetes and heart-related disease.

The history of the Mediterranean diet?

Mediterranean diet is one of the oldest diets plans popular in worldwide. It is near about more than three thousand years old diet plan. Mediterranean is the name of the sea situated between Asia, Europe and Africa. Mediterranean diet is an eating habit of people's lives around the coast of the Mediterranean Sea like Italy, France, Spain, Greece and Morocco. There are near about 22 countries situated near the Mediterranean Sea. The large amounts of seasonable fruits are available during four seasons because of mild climate.

There are large numbers of olive trees found in Mediterranean regions. Near about 90 percent of the world, olive trees are grown in Mediterranean regions. Due to large sea coast fishing is the main occupation by most of the people in this region and fish is part of the

Mediterranean diet. Most of the scientific study conducted over Mediterranean diet proves that the diet helps to reduce the all-cause mortality. It also reduces the risk of heart-related disease and early death.

The Science Behind Mediterranean diet

Mediterranean diet is one of the high-fat diets that allow near about 40 percent of calories from fat. It is the most studied and healthiest diet worldwide.

The scientific research and study show that the peoples who follow the Mediterranean diet have lower the risk of cardiac mortality and heart disease. The study shows that the Mediterranean diet is a high-fat diet; during the diet, our body consumes a high intake of unsaturated fat and low intake of saturated fat. Unsaturated fats help to increase the HDL (Good Cholesterol) level into your body. Olive oil is one of the main fats used during the Mediterranean diet. Olive oils are full of monounsaturated fats that help to control your diabetes. It improves your insulin sensitivity and controls your diabetes. If you don't have diabetes then it helps to reduce the risk of developing diabetes.

Another study shows that the Mediterranean diet reduces the risk of stomach cancer and also reducing the risk of breast cancer in women.

Benefits of the Mediterranean diet

Mediterranean diet is one of the oldest diets in the world comes with various types of health benefits. Some of the important benefits are as follows.

- **Improves heart health**

During the Mediterranean diet, olive oil is used as a primary fat. This olive oil contains healthy fat known as monounsaturated fat helps to increase the HDL (Good Cholesterol) level and reduce the LDL (Bad Cholesterol) level. Fish is also part of the Mediterranean lifestyle, fish contains Omega-3 fatty acid which helps to improve the heart health and reduce the risk of heart failure, strokes, and sudden cardiac death.

- **Help to maintain blood sugar level**

According to the American Heart Association, the Mediterranean diet is low in sugar. It is very effective in type-2 diabetes patients and helps to maintain the blood sugar level. Mediterranean diet is rich in monounsaturated fats which help to reduce the cholesterol level and maintain your blood sugar level.

- **Increase your lifespan**

Mediterranean region's climate is clear and pollution-free climate. Due to this, you have to find fresh vegetables, seasonable fruits, beans, olives and fish in this region. All of the natural and fresh foods are full of antioxidants, which helps to reduce the inflammation in your body and slow down your aging process. It also reduces the risk of heart-related disease, inflammation, Alzheimer's and depression. The peoples live in Mediterranean regions have a longer lifespan.

- **Protects from cancer**

Mediterranean diet is one of the simple plant-based food diet. It allows high fat moderate protein and low consumption of red meat. Most of the scientific study and research show that reduction of red meat from your diet and increase the consumption of olive oil and fish into your daily diet will help to reduce the risk of several common cancers. Fish contains omega-3 fatty acids which reduce the risk of cancer.

- **Fight against depression**

The foods associated with the Mediterranean diet have anti-inflammatory properties which help to reduce the depression and help to improve your mood. One of the scientific research studies shows that the peoples who follow the Mediterranean diet have 98.6 percent of lower the risk of depression.

Chapter 2: Breakfast & Brunch

Date Apple Oats

Preparation Time: 10 minutes
Cooking Time: 4 minutes
Serve: 2

Ingredients:

- 1/4 cup oats
- 1/4 tsp vanilla
- 14 tsp cinnamon
- 2 dates, chopped
- 1 apple, chopped
- 1/2 cup water

Directions:

1. Spray instant pot from inside with cooking spray.
2. Add all ingredients to the instant pot and stir well.
3. Seal pot with lid and cook on high for 4 minutes.
4. Once done, allow to release pressure naturally for 10 minutes then release remaining using quick release. Remove lid.
5. Stir well and serve.

Nutritional Value (Amount per Serving):

- Calories 161
- Fat 1.1 g
- Carbohydrates 41.6 g
- Sugar 17.4 g
- Protein 2.5 g
- Cholesterol 0 mg

Healthy Cauliflower Mushroom Salad

Preparation Time: 10 minutes

Cooking Time: 20 minutes

Serve: 2

Ingredients:

- 1 cup cauliflower rice
- 1 tbsp chives, chopped
- 1 cup vegetable stock
- 1 tbsp garlic, minced
- 2 tbsp fresh lemon juice
- 2 cups mushrooms, sliced
- 2 tbsp olive oil
- 1 small onion, chopped
- 1/4 cup grape tomatoes, halved
- Pepper
- Salt

Directions:

1. Add oil into the inner pot of instant pot and set the pot on sauté mode.
2. Add garlic, onion, and mushrooms and sauté for 5 minutes.
3. Add remaining ingredients and stir well.
4. Seal pot with lid and cook on high for 15 minutes.
5. Once done, allow to release pressure naturally for 10 minutes then release remaining using quick release. Remove lid.
6. Stir well and serve.

Nutritional Value (Amount per Serving):

- Calories 97
- Fat 7.7 g
- Carbohydrates 6 g
- Sugar 3 g
- Protein 2.7 g
- Cholesterol 0 mg

Pepper Chickpea Salad

Preparation Time: 10 minutes

Cooking Time: 15 minutes

Serve: 2

Ingredients:

- 2 cups chickpeas, soaked overnight & drained
- 3 tbsp olive oil
- 1/4 cup balsamic vinegar
- 1 tbsp chives, chopped
- 1 onion, chopped
- 2 celery stalks, chopped
- 1 carrot, chopped
- 1/2 tsp chili powder
- 1 tsp paprika
- 1 1/2 cups bell pepper, chopped
- 1/2 tsp garlic, minced
- 3 cups vegetable stock
- Pepper
- Salt

Directions:

1. Add all ingredients into the inner pot of instant pot and stir well.
2. Seal pot with lid and cook on high for 15 minutes.
3. Once done, allow to release pressure naturally for 10 minutes then release remaining using quick release. Remove lid.
4. Stir well and serve.

Nutritional Value (Amount per Serving):

- Calories 498
- Fat 16.9 g
- Carbohydrates 69.8 g
- Sugar 15.7 g
- Protein 20.7 g
- Cholesterol 0 mg

Quinoa Breakfast Bowls

Preparation Time: 10 minutes

Cooking Time: 4 minutes

Serve: 2

Ingredients:

- 1 cup quinoa, rinsed and drained
- 1 cucumber, chopped
- 1 red bell pepper, chopped
- 1/2 cup olives, pitted and sliced
- 1 tbsp fresh basil, chopped
- 2 tbsp fresh lemon juice
- 1 tsp lemon zest, grated
- 1 1/2 cups water
- Pepper
- Salt

Directions:

1. Add quinoa, lemon zest, lemon juice, water, pepper, and salt into the instant pot and stir well.
2. Seal pot with lid and cook on high for 4 minutes.
3. Once done, allow to release pressure naturally for 10 minutes then release remaining using quick release. Remove lid.
4. Add remaining ingredients and stir well.
5. Serve immediately and enjoy it.

Nutritional Value (Amount per Serving):

- Calories 199
- Fat 4.6 g
- Carbohydrates 33.6 g
- Sugar 3 g
- Protein 7 g
- Cholesterol 0 mg

Breakfast Rice Bowls

Preparation Time: 10 minutes

Cooking Time: 20 minutes

Serve: 2

Ingredients:

- 1 cup of brown rice
- 1 tbsp fresh basil, chopped
- 1/4 cup salsa
- 3/4 cup olives, pitted and sliced
- 1 tbsp olive oil
- 1 onion, chopped
- 2 cups vegetable stock
- Pepper
- Salt

Directions:

1. Add oil into the inner pot of instant pot and set the pot on sauté mode.
2. Add onion and sauté for 2 minutes.
3. Add rice and cook for 3 minutes.
4. Add remaining ingredients and stir well.
5. Seal pot with lid and cook on high for 15 minutes.
6. Once done, allow to release pressure naturally for 10 minutes then release remaining using quick release. Remove lid.
7. Stir well and serve.

Nutritional Value (Amount per Serving):

- Calories 250
- Fat 7.6 g
- Carbohydrates 41.8 g
- Sugar 2 g
- Protein 4.5 g
- Cholesterol 0 mg

Spinach Egg Breakfast

Preparation Time: 10 minutes

Cooking Time: 8 minutes

Serve: 2

Ingredients:

- 6 eggs
- 1 tomato, chopped
- 1/2 cup mozzarella cheese, shredded
- 1 cup spinach, chopped
- 1/4 cup feta cheese, crumbled
- Pepper
- Salt

Directions:

1. Pour 1 cup of water into the instant pot then place the steamer rack in the pot.
2. In a bowl, whisk eggs with pepper and salt. Add remaining ingredients and stir well.
3. Spray heat-safe dish with cooking spray. Pour egg mixture into the prepared dish and place dish on top of the steamer rack.
4. Seal pot with lid and cook on high for 8 minutes.
5. Once done, release pressure using quick release. Remove lid.
6. Serve and enjoy.

Nutritional Value (Amount per Serving):

- Calories 267
- Fat 18.5 g
- Carbohydrates 3.8 g
- Sugar 2.7 g
- Protein 22 g
- Cholesterol 511 mg

Simple Breakfast Quinoa

Preparation Time: 10 minutes
Cooking Time: 1 minute
Serve: 2

Ingredients:
- 1 1/2 cups quinoa, rinsed and drained
- 2 1/2 cups water
- 1/2 tsp vanilla
- 2 tbsp maple syrup
- 1/4 tsp ground cinnamon
- Pinch of salt

Directions:
1. Spray instant pot from inside with cooking spray.
2. Add all ingredients into the instant pot and stir well.
3. Seal pot with lid and cook on high for 1 minute.
4. Once done, allow to release pressure naturally for 10 minutes then release remaining using quick release. Remove lid.
5. Fluff quinoa using fork and serve.

Nutritional Value (Amount per Serving):
- Calories 175
- Fat 2.6 g
- Carbohydrates 31.9 g
- Sugar 4 g
- Protein 6 g
- Cholesterol 0 mg

Simple Lemon Quinoa

Preparation Time: 10 minutes

Cooking Time: 1 minute

Serve: 2

Ingredients:

- 2 cups quinoa, rinsed and drained
- 1 fresh lemon juice
- 2 tbsp fresh parsley, chopped
- 3 cups of water
- 1/4 tsp salt

Directions:

1. Spray instant pot from inside with cooking spray.
2. Add all ingredients except lemon juice and parsley into the pot. Stir well.
3. Seal pot with lid and cook on high for 1 minute.
4. Once done, allow to release pressure naturally for 10 minutes then release remaining using quick release. Remove lid.
5. Add parsley and lemon juice.
6. Stir and serve.

Nutritional Value (Amount per Serving):

- Calories 317
- Fat 5.3 g
- Carbohydrates 54.9 g
- Sugar 0.3 g
- Protein 12.2 g
- Cholesterol 0 mg

Chapter 3: Soups & Stews

Chicken Rice Soup

Preparation Time: 10 minutes
Cooking Time: 9 minutes
Serve: 2

Ingredients:

- 1 lb chicken breast, boneless
- 2 thyme sprigs
- 1 tsp garlic, chopped
- 1/4 tsp turmeric
- 1 tbsp olive oil
- 2 tbsp fresh parsley, chopped
- 2 tbsp fresh lemon juice
- 1/4 cup rice
- 1/2 cup celery, diced
- 1/2 cup onion, chopped
- 2 carrots, chopped
- 5 cups vegetable stock
- Pepper
- Salt

Directions:

1. Add oil into the inner pot of instant pot and set the pot on sauté mode.
2. Add garlic, onion, carrots, and celery and sauté for 3 minutes.
3. Add the rest of the ingredients and stir well.
4. Seal pot with lid and cook on high for 6 minutes.
5. Once done, release pressure using quick release. Remove lid.
6. Shred chicken using a fork.
7. Serve and enjoy.

Nutritional Value (Amount per Serving):

- Calories 237
- Fat 6.8 g
- Carbohydrates 16.6 g
- Sugar 3.4 g
- Protein 26.2 g
- Cholesterol 73 mg

Easy & Delicious Beef Stew

Preparation Time: 10 minutes

Cooking Time: 30 minutes

Serve: 2

Ingredients:

- 1 1/2 lbs beef stew meat, cut into cubed
- 1/2 cup sweet corn
- 1 cup can tomato, crushed
- 1 cup chicken stock
- 4 carrots, chopped
- 1 onion, chopped
- 1 tbsp olive oil
- Pepper
- Salt

Directions:

1. Add oil into the inner pot of instant pot and set the pot on sauté mode.
2. Add onion and meat and sauté for 5 minutes.
3. Add remaining ingredients and stir well.
4. Seal pot with lid and cook on high pressure 25 for minutes.
5. Once done, allow to release pressure naturally for 10 minutes then release remaining using quick release. Remove lid.
6. Stir and serve.

Nutritional Value (Amount per Serving):

- Calories 410
- Fat 14.4 g
- Carbohydrates 14 g
- Sugar 4.8 g
- Protein 54.4 g
- Cholesterol 152 mg

Creamy Chicken Soup

Preparation Time: 10 minutes

Cooking Time: 10 minutes

Serve: 2

Ingredients:

- 2 lbs chicken breast, boneless and cut into chunks
- 8 oz cream cheese
- 2 tbsp taco seasoning
- 1 cup of salsa
- 2 cups chicken stock
- 28 oz can tomatoes, diced
- Salt

Directions:

1. Add all ingredients except cream cheese into the instant pot.
2. Seal pot with lid and cook on high pressure 10 for minutes.
3. Once done, allow to release pressure naturally. Remove lid.
4. Remove chicken from pot and shred using a fork. Return shredded chicken to the pot.
5. Add cream cheese and stir well.
6. Serve and enjoy.

Nutritional Value (Amount per Serving):

- Calories 471
- Fat 24.1 g
- Carbohydrates 19.6 g
- Sugar 6.2 g
- Protein 43.9 g
- Cholesterol 157 mg

Simple Black Bean Soup

Preparation Time: 10 minutes

Cooking Time: 40 minutes

Serve: 2

Ingredients:

- 1 lb black beans, soaked overnight
- 1 tbsp olive oil
- 1 tbsp fresh parsley, chopped
- 1 onion, chopped
- 7 cups vegetable stock
- 2 tbsp vinegar
- Pepper
- Salt

Directions:

1. Add all ingredients except parsley and vinegar into the instant pot and stir well.
2. Seal pot with lid and cook on high pressure 40 for minutes.
3. Once done, allow to release pressure naturally for 10 minutes then release remaining using quick release. Remove lid.
4. Stir in parsley and vinegar and serve.

Nutritional Value (Amount per Serving):

- Calories 220
- Fat 2.7 g
- Carbohydrates 37.5 g
- Sugar 2.4 g
- Protein 12.8 g
- Cholesterol 0 mg

Celery Soup

Preparation Time: 10 minutes

Cooking Time: 30 minutes

Serve: 2

Ingredients:

- 6 cups celery stalk, chopped
- 1 cup heavy cream
- 1 onion, chopped
- 2 cups vegetable broth
- 1/2 tsp dill
- Salt

Directions:

1. Add all ingredients into the instant pot and stir well.
2. Seal pot with lid and cook on high for 30 minutes.
3. Once done, release pressure using quick release. Remove lid.
4. Blend soup using an immersion blender until smooth.
5. Serve and enjoy.

Nutritional Value (Amount per Serving):

- Calories 158
- Fat 12.1 g
- Carbohydrates 8.4 g
- Sugar 3.6 g
- Protein 4.4 g
- Cholesterol 41 mg

Nutritious Kidney Bean Soup

Preparation Time: 10 minutes

Cooking Time: 1 hour 40 minutes

Serve: 2

Ingredients:

- 3 cups red kidney beans, soaked overnight & drain
- 1/4 cup fresh parsley, chopped
- 6 cups of water
- 1/4 cup olive oil
- 1 1/2 tbsp tomato paste
- 2 bell peppers, chopped
- 2 carrots, chopped
- 1 tbsp garlic, minced
- 1 onion, chopped
- 1 tsp salt

Directions:

1. Add oil into the inner pot of instant pot and set the pot on sauté mode.
2. Add garlic and onion and sauté until onion is softened.
3. Add carrots and bell peppers and sauté for 3-5 minutes.
4. Add beans, parsley, tomato paste, water, and salt and stir everything well.
5. Seal pot with lid and cook on high for 1 hour 40 minutes.
6. Once done, release pressure using quick release. Remove lid.
7. Stir well and serve.

Nutritional Value (Amount per Serving):

- Calories 312
- Fat 7.2 g
- Carbohydrates 48.4 g
- Sugar 4.7 g
- Protein 16.4 g
- Cholesterol 0 mg

Pepper Pumpkin Soup

Preparation Time: 10 minutes

Cooking Time: 6 minutes

Serve: 2

Ingredients:
- 2 cups pumpkin puree
- 1 onion, chopped
- 4 cups vegetable broth
- 1/4 tsp nutmeg
- 1/4 cup red bell pepper, chopped
- 1/8 tsp thyme, dried
- 1/2 tsp salt

Directions:
1. Add all ingredients into the instant pot and stir well.
2. Seal pot with lid and cook on high for 6 minutes.
3. Once done, allow to release pressure naturally for 5 minutes then release remaining using quick release. Remove lid.
4. Blend soup using an immersion blender until smooth.
5. Serve and enjoy.

Nutritional Value (Amount per Serving):
- Calories 63
- Fat 1.2 g
- Carbohydrates 9.4 g
- Sugar 4.2 g
- Protein 4.4 g
- Cholesterol 0 mg

Creamy Squash Cauliflower Soup

Preparation Time: 10 minutes

Cooking Time: 8 minutes

Serve: 2

Ingredients:

- 1 cauliflower head, cut into florets
- 1 bell pepper, diced
- 1 small butternut squash, peeled and chopped
- 1/2 tsp dried parsley
- 1/2 tsp dried mix herbs
- 1 cup vegetable stock
- 1/4 cup yogurt
- 1 onion, chopped
- Pepper
- Salt

Directions:

1. Add all ingredients except yogurt into the instant pot.
2. Seal pot with lid and cook on high for 8 minutes.
3. Once done, release pressure using quick release. Remove lid.
4. Stir in yogurt and blend soup using an immersion blender until smooth.
5. Serve and enjoy.

Nutritional Value (Amount per Serving):

- Calories 54
- Fat 0.3 g
- Carbohydrates 11.3 g
- Sugar 4.4 g
- Protein 2.5 g
- Cholesterol 1 mg

Chapter 4: Pasta, Grains & Beans

Garlic Onion Pinto Beans

Preparation Time: 10 minutes
Cooking Time: 30 minutes
Serve: 2

Ingredients:

- 3 cups dry pinto beans, soaked overnight
- 6 cups vegetable stock
- 2 tsp dried oregano
- 1/3 cup dried onion
- 2 tbsp dried garlic
- 1 tsp sea salt

Directions:

1. Add all ingredients into the inner pot of instant pot and stir well.
2. Seal pot with lid and cook on high for 30 minutes.
3. Once done, allow to release pressure naturally. Remove lid.
4. Serve and enjoy.

Nutritional Value (Amount per Serving):

- Calories 262
- Fat 1 g
- Carbohydrates 47.3 g
- Sugar 2.3 g
- Protein 16 g
- Cholesterol 0 mg

Mac & Cheese

Preparation Time: 10 minutes

Cooking Time: 4 minutes

Serve: 2

Ingredients:

- 1 lb whole grain pasta
- 1/2 cup parmesan cheese, grated
- 4 cups cheddar cheese, shredded
- 1 cup milk
- 1/4 tsp garlic powder
- 1/2 tsp ground mustard
- 2 tbsp olive oil
- 4 cups of water
- Pepper
- Salt

Directions:

1. Add pasta, garlic powder, mustard, oil, water, pepper, and salt into the instant pot.
2. Seal pot with lid and cook on high for 4 minutes.
3. Once done, release pressure using quick release. Remove lid.
4. Add remaining ingredients and stir well and serve.

Nutritional Value (Amount per Serving):

- Calories 509
- Fat 25.7 g
- Carbohydrates 43.8 g
- Sugar 3.8 g
- Protein 27.3 g
- Cholesterol 66 mg

Delicious Pasta Primavera

Preparation Time: 10 minutes
Cooking Time: 4 minutes
Serve: 2

Ingredients:
- 8 oz whole wheat penne pasta
- 1 tbsp fresh lemon juice
- 2 tbsp fresh parsley, chopped
- 1/4 cup almonds slivered
- 1/4 cup parmesan cheese, grated
- 14 oz can tomatoes, diced
- 1/2 cup prunes
- 1/2 cup zucchini, chopped
- 1/2 cup asparagus, cut into 1-inch pieces
- 1/2 cup carrots, chopped
- 1/2 cup broccoli, chopped
- 1 3/4 cups vegetable stock
- Pepper
- Salt

Directions:
1. Add stock, pars, tomatoes, prunes, zucchini, asparagus, carrots, and broccoli into the instant pot and stir well.
2. Seal pot with lid and cook on high for 4 minutes.
3. Once done, release pressure using quick release. Remove lid.
4. Add remaining ingredients and stir well and serve.

Nutritional Value (Amount per Serving):
- Calories 303
- Fat 2.6 g
- Carbohydrates 63.5 g
- Sugar 13.4 g
- Protein 12.8 g
- Cholesterol 1 mg

Pesto Chicken Pasta

Preparation Time: 10 minutes
Cooking Time: 10 minutes
Serve: 2

Ingredients:

- 1 lb chicken breast, skinless, boneless, and diced
- 3 tbsp olive oil
- 1/2 cup parmesan cheese, shredded
- 1 tsp Italian seasoning
- 1/4 cup heavy cream
- 16 oz whole wheat pasta
- 6 oz basil pesto
- 3 1/2 cups water
- Pepper
- Salt

Directions:

1. Season chicken with Italian seasoning, pepper, and salt.
2. Add oil into the inner pot of instant pot and set the pot on sauté mode.
3. Add chicken to the pot and sauté until brown.
4. Add remaining ingredients except for parmesan cheese, heavy cream, and pesto and stir well.
5. Seal pot with lid and cook on high for 5 minutes.
6. Once done, release pressure using quick release. Remove lid.
7. Stir in parmesan cheese, heavy cream, and pesto and serve.

Nutritional Value (Amount per Serving):

- Calories 475
- Fat 14.7 g
- Carbohydrates 57 g
- Sugar 2.8 g
- Protein 28.7 g
- Cholesterol 61 mg

Corn Risotto

Preparation Time: 10 minutes
Cooking Time: 12 minutes
Serve: 2

Ingredients:

- 1 cup of rice
- 3 cups vegetable broth
- 1 tbsp olive oil
- 1 tsp garlic, minced
- 1 onion, chopped
- 3/4 cup sweet corn
- 1 red pepper, diced
- 1 tsp dried mix herbs
- 1/4 tsp pepper
- 1/2 tsp salt

Directions:

1. Add oil into the inner pot of instant pot and set the pot on sauté mode.
2. Add onion and garlic and sauté for 5 minutes.
3. Add the rest of the ingredients and stir well.
4. Seal pot with lid and cook on high for 8 minutes.
5. Once done, release pressure using quick release. Remove lid.
6. Stir well and serve.

Nutritional Value (Amount per Serving):

- Calories 304
- Fat 5.3 g
- Carbohydrates 54.5 g
- Sugar 4.7 g
- Protein 9.5 g
- Cholesterol 0 mg

Chicken Risotto

Preparation Time: 10 minutes

Cooking Time: 12 minutes

Serve: 2

Ingredients:

- 1 lb chicken breasts, skinless, boneless, and cut into chunks
- 3 tbsp fresh parsley, chopped
- 1/3 cup parmesan cheese, grated
- 1 cup of rice
- 2 cups chicken stock
- 1 cup mushrooms, sliced
- 1 cup onion, diced
- 2 tbsp olive oil

Directions:

1. Add oil into the inner pot of instant pot and set the pot on sauté mode.
2. Add chicken and cook for 3 minutes.
3. Add mushrooms and onions and cook for 2 minutes.
4. Add remaining ingredients except for cheese and stir well.
5. Seal pot with lid and cook on high for 7 minutes.
6. Once done, release pressure using quick release. Remove lid.
7. Stir well and serve.

Nutritional Value (Amount per Serving):

- Calories 490
- Fat 17.7 g
- Carbohydrates 41.1 g
- Sugar 2 g
- Protein 39.8 g
- Cholesterol 106 mg

Delicious Chicken Pasta

Preparation Time: 10 minutes

Cooking Time: 17 minutes

Serve: 2

Ingredients:

- 3 chicken breasts, skinless, boneless, cut into pieces
- 9 oz whole-grain pasta
- 1/2 cup olives, sliced
- 1/2 cup sun-dried tomatoes
- 1 tbsp roasted red peppers, chopped
- 14 oz can tomatoes, diced
- 2 cups marinara sauce
- 1 cup chicken broth
- Pepper
- Salt

Directions:

1. Add all ingredients except whole-grain pasta into the instant pot and stir well.
2. Seal pot with lid and cook on high for 12 minutes.
3. Once done, allow to release pressure naturally. Remove lid.
4. Add pasta and stir well. Seal pot again and select manual and set timer for 5 minutes.
5. Once done, allow to release pressure naturally for 5 minutes then release remaining using quick release. Remove lid.
6. Stir well and serve.

Nutritional Value (Amount per Serving):

- Calories 615
- Fat 15.4 g
- Carbohydrates 71 g
- Sugar 17.6 g
- Protein 48 g
- Cholesterol 100 mg

Creamy & Tasty Risotto

Preparation Time: 10 minutes

Cooking Time: 7 minutes

Serve: 2

Ingredients:

- 2 cups of rice
- 1/2 cup mozzarella cheese, shredded
- 1 cup parmesan cheese, shredded
- 4 cups vegetable stock
- 1/2 cup wine
- 1 small onion, chopped
- 2 tbsp olive oil
- Salt

Directions:

1. Add oil into the inner pot of instant pot and set the pot on sauté mode.
2. Add onion and sauté for 2 minutes.
3. Add rice, wine, stock, and salt and stir well.
4. Seal pot with lid and cook on high for 5 minutes.
5. Once done, release pressure using quick release. Remove lid.
6. Add cheeses and stir until cheese is melted.
7. Serve and enjoy.

Nutritional Value (Amount per Serving):

- Calories 517
- Fat 13.2 g
- Carbohydrates 78.2 g
- Sugar 1.8 g
- Protein 15.4 g
- Cholesterol 18 mg

Chapter 5: Vegetables

Italian Tomato Mushrooms

Preparation Time: 10 minutes

Cooking Time: 13 minutes

Serve: 2

Ingredients:

- 1 cup tomatoes, chopped
- 2 cups mushrooms, sliced
- 1 tbsp olive oil
- 1/2 cup zucchini, chopped
- 1/4 cup green onions, chopped
- 1 cup cream cheese
- 1/2 tsp mint, chopped
- 1/2 tsp dried rosemary
- 1/2 tsp dried oregano
- Salt

Directions:

1. Add tomatoes, rosemary, oregano, mint, and salt into the blender and blend until smooth.
2. Add oil into the inner pot of instant pot and set the pot on sauté mode.
3. Add green onion and zucchini and sauté for 5 minutes. Transfer zucchini and onion mixture on a plate.
4. Add 1 cup water and mushrooms into the pot and stir well.
5. Seal pot with lid and cook on high for 3 minutes.
6. Once done, release pressure using quick release. Remove lid.
7. Add blended tomato mixture, zucchini, and cream cheese and cook on sauté mode for 5 minutes.
8. Stir well and serve.

Nutritional Value (Amount per Serving):

- Calories 507
- Fat 48 g
- Carbohydrates 11.2 g
- Sugar 4.6 g
- Protein 12.4 g
- Cholesterol 128 mg

Delicious Cauliflower Rice

Preparation Time: 10 minutes
Cooking Time: 15 minutes
Serve: 2

Ingredients:

- 1 1/2 cups cauliflower rice
- 1/2 tsp dried thyme
- 1 tsp paprika
- 2 eggplant, cut into chunks
- 1 tbsp olive oil
- 2 cups vegetable stock
- 1 onion, chopped
- 1/2 cup grape tomatoes
- Pepper
- Salt

Directions:

1. Add oil into the inner pot of instant pot and set the pot on sauté mode.
2. Add onion and sauté for 3 minutes.
3. Add remaining ingredients and stir everything well.
4. Seal pot with lid and cook on high for 12 minutes.
5. Once done, allow to release pressure naturally for 10 minutes then release remaining using quick release. Remove lid.
6. Stir well and serve.

Nutritional Value (Amount per Serving):

- Calories 128
- Fat 4.8 g
- Carbohydrates 20.3 g
- Sugar 10.5 g
- Protein 4.5 g
- Cholesterol 0 mg

Healthy Vegetable Medley

Preparation Time: 10 minutes

Cooking Time: 17 minutes

Serve: 2

Ingredients:

- 3 cups broccoli florets
- 1 sweet potato, chopped
- 1 tsp garlic, minced
- 14 oz coconut milk
- 28 oz can tomatoes, chopped
- 14 oz can chickpeas, drained and rinsed
- 1 onion, chopped
- 1 tbsp olive oil
- 1 tsp Italian seasoning
- Pepper
- Salt

Directions:

1. Add oil into the inner pot of instant pot and set the pot on sauté mode.
2. Add garlic and onion and sauté until onion is softened.
3. Add remaining ingredients and stir everything well.
4. Seal pot with lid and cook on high for 12 minutes.
5. Once done, allow to release pressure naturally for 10 minutes then release remaining using quick release. Remove lid.
6. Stir well and serve.

Nutritional Value (Amount per Serving):

- Calories 322
- Fat 19.3 g
- Carbohydrates 34.3 g
- Sugar 9.6 g
- Protein 7.9 g
- Cholesterol 1 mg

Healthy Chickpea & Broccoli

Preparation Time: 10 minutes

Cooking Time: 5 minutes

Serve: 2

Ingredients:

- 14 oz can chickpeas, rinsed and drained
- 1 tbsp olive oil
- 4 cups broccoli florets, chopped
- 1 tbsp garlic, chopped
- 1/4 cup vegetable stock
- 1/4 tsp red pepper flakes
- Pepper
- Salt

Directions:

1. Add oil into the inner pot of instant pot and set the pot on sauté mode.
2. Add garlic and sauté for 30 seconds.
3. Add remaining ingredients and stir well.
4. Seal pot with lid and cook on high for 5 minutes.
5. Once done, allow to release pressure naturally for 10 minutes then release remaining using quick release. Remove lid.
6. Stir and serve.

Nutritional Value (Amount per Serving):

- Calories 366
- Fat 9.9 g
- Carbohydrates 58.6 g
- Sugar 3.2 g
- Protein 15.3 g
- Cholesterol 0 mg

Creamy Lemon Bell Peppers

Preparation Time: 10 minutes

Cooking Time: 15 minutes

Serve: 2

Ingredients:
- 1 lb bell peppers, cut into strips
- 1 tbsp chives, chopped
- 1 tbsp fresh lime juice
- 1/2 cup heavy cream
- 1/4 tsp dried mix herbs
- Pepper
- Salt

Directions:
1. Add all ingredients into the inner pot of instant pot and stir well.
2. Seal pot with lid and cook on high for 15 minutes.
3. Once done, allow to release pressure naturally for 5 minutes then release remaining using quick release. Remove lid.
4. Stir and serve.

Nutritional Value (Amount per Serving):
- Calories 72
- Fat 5.7 g
- Carbohydrates 5.2 g
- Sugar 1.8 g
- Protein 0.9 g
- Cholesterol 21 mg

Creamy Dill Potatoes

Preparation Time: 10 minutes

Cooking Time: 20 minutes

Serve: 2

Ingredients:

- 2 lbs potatoes, peeled and cut into chunks
- 1 tbsp fresh dill, chopped
- 1 cup vegetable stock
- 3/4 cup heavy cream
- Pepper
- Salt

Directions:

1. Add all ingredients into the inner pot of instant pot and stir well.
2. Seal pot with lid and cook on high for 20 minutes.
3. Once done, allow to release pressure naturally for 10 minutes then release remaining using quick release. Remove lid.
4. Stir and serve.

Nutritional Value (Amount per Serving):

- Calories 238
- Fat 8.6 g
- Carbohydrates 37 g
- Sugar 2.8 g
- Protein 4.5 g
- Cholesterol 31 mg

Potato Salad

Preparation Time: 10 minutes

Cooking Time: 10 minutes

Serve: 2

Ingredients:

- 5 cups potato, cubed
- 1/4 cup fresh parsley, chopped
- 1/4 tsp red pepper flakes
- 1 tbsp olive oil
- 1/3 cup mayonnaise
- 1/2 tbsp oregano
- 2 tbsp capers
- 3/4 cup feta cheese, crumbled
- 1 cup olives, halved
- 3 cups of water
- 3/4 cup onion, chopped
- Pepper
- Salt

Directions:

1. Add potatoes, onion, and salt into the instant pot.
2. Seal pot with lid and cook on high for 3 minutes.
3. Once done, release pressure using quick release. Remove lid.
4. Remove potatoes from pot and place in a large mixing bowl.
5. Add remaining ingredients and stir everything well.
6. Serve and enjoy.

Nutritional Value (Amount per Serving):

- Calories 152
- Fat 9.9 g
- Carbohydrates 13.6 g
- Sugar 2.1 g
- Protein 3.5 g
- Cholesterol 15 mg

Radish & Asparagus

Preparation Time: 10 minutes
Cooking Time: 8 minutes
Serve: 2

Ingredients:

- 3/4 cup radishes, halved
- 1 lb asparagus, trimmed & cut in half
- 1 tsp chili powder
- 1 tsp lemon zest, grated
- 2 tbsp green onion, chopped
- 2 tbsp olive oil
- Pepper
- Salt

Directions:

1. Add all ingredients into the inner pot of instant pot and stir well.
2. Seal pot with lid and cook on high for 8 minutes.
3. Once done, allow to release pressure naturally for 5 minutes then release remaining using quick release. Remove lid.
4. Stir and serve.

Nutritional Value (Amount per Serving):

- Calories 90
- Fat 7.3 g
- Carbohydrates 5.8 g
- Sugar 2.7 g
- Protein 2.8 g
- Cholesterol 0 mg

Chapter 6: Appetizers

Spicy Jalapeno Spinach Artichoke Dip

Preparation Time: 10 minutes

Cooking Time: 3 minutes

Serve: 2

Ingredients:

- 10 oz spinach, chopped
- 1/2 cup parmesan cheese, grated
- 8 oz Italian cheese, shredded
- 1/4 cup fresh parsley, chopped
- 2 tbsp jalapeno, diced
- 1 1/2 tbsp garlic, minced
- 2 tbsp green onion, chopped
- 14 oz cream cheese, cubed
- 18 oz jar marinated artichoke hearts, chopped
- 1 1/2 tbsp fresh lemon juice
- 1/2 cup vegetable stock

Directions:

1. Add all ingredients except parmesan cheese and Italian cheese into the instant pot and stir well.
2. Seal pot with lid and cook on high for 3 minutes.
3. Once done, allow to release pressure naturally for 5 minutes then release remaining using quick release. Remove lid.
4. Set pot on sauté mode. Add parmesan cheese and Italian cheese and stir well and cook until cheese is melted.
5. Serve and enjoy.

Nutritional Value (Amount per Serving):

- Calories 195
- Fat 16.3 g
- Carbohydrates 3.7 g
- Sugar 0.6 g
- Protein 6.7 g
- Cholesterol 42 mg

Olive Eggplant Spread

Preparation Time: 10 minutes

Cooking Time: 8 minutes

Serve: 2

Ingredients:

- 1 3/4 lbs eggplant, chopped
- 1/2 tbsp dried oregano
- 1/4 cup olives, pitted and chopped
- 1 tbsp tahini
- 1/4 cup fresh lime juice
- 1/2 cup water
- 2 garlic cloves
- 1/4 cup olive oil
- Salt

Directions:

1. Add oil into the inner pot of instant pot and set the pot on sauté mode.
2. Add eggplant and cook for 3-5 minutes. Turn off sauté mode.
3. Add water and salt and stir well.
4. Seal pot with lid and cook on high for 3 minutes.
5. Once done, release pressure using quick release. Remove lid.
6. Drain eggplant well and transfer into the food processor.
7. Add remaining ingredients into the food processor and process until smooth.
8. Serve and enjoy.

Nutritional Value (Amount per Serving):

- Calories 65
- Fat 5.3 g
- Carbohydrates 4.7 g
- Sugar 2 g
- Protein 0.9 g
- Cholesterol 0 mg

Pinto Bean Dip

Preparation Time: 10 minutes

Cooking Time: 45 minutes

Serve: 2

Ingredients:

- 1 cup dry pinto beans
- 2 tsp chili powder
- 3 chilies de Arbol, remove the stem
- 4 cups of water
- 1 tsp salt

Directions:

1. Add beans, chilies, and water into the instant pot and stir well.
2. Seal pot with lid and cook on high for 45 minutes.
3. Once done, allow to release pressure naturally for 10 minutes then release remaining using quick release. Remove lid.
4. Transfer instant pot bean mixture into the blender along with chili powder and salt and blend until smooth.
5. Serve and enjoy.

Nutritional Value (Amount per Serving):

- Calories 139
- Fat 0.6 g
- Carbohydrates 24.6 g
- Sugar 4.2 g
- Protein 8 g
- Cholesterol 0 mg

Homemade Salsa

Preparation Time: 10 minutes

Cooking Time: 5 minutes

Serve: 2

Ingredients:

- 12 oz grape tomatoes, halved
- 1/4 cup fresh cilantro, chopped
- 1 fresh lime juice
- 28 oz tomatoes, crushed
- 1 tbsp garlic, minced
- 1 green bell pepper, chopped
- 1 red bell pepper, chopped
- 2 onions, chopped
- 6 whole tomatoes
- Salt

Directions:

1. Add whole tomatoes into the instant pot and gently smash the tomatoes.
2. Add remaining ingredients except cilantro, lime juice, and salt and stir well.
3. Seal pot with lid and cook on high for 5 minutes.
4. Once done, allow to release pressure naturally for 10 minutes then release remaining using quick release. Remove lid.
5. Add cilantro, lime juice, and salt and stir well.
6. Serve and enjoy.

Nutritional Value (Amount per Serving):

- Calories 146
- Fat 1.2 g
- Carbohydrates 33.2 g
- Sugar 4 g
- Protein 6.9 g
- Cholesterol 0 mg

Flavorful Roasted Baby Potatoes

Preparation Time: 10 minutes

Cooking Time: 10 minutes

Serve: 2

Ingredients:

- 2 lbs baby potatoes, clean and cut in half
- 1/2 cup vegetable stock
- 1 tsp paprika
- 3/4 tsp garlic powder
- 1 tsp onion powder
- 2 tsp Italian seasoning
- 1 tbsp olive oil
- Pepper
- Salt

Directions:

1. Add oil into the inner pot of instant pot and set the pot on sauté mode.
2. Add potatoes and sauté for 5 minutes. Add remaining ingredients and stir well.
3. Seal pot with lid and cook on high for 5 minutes.
4. Once done, release pressure using quick release. Remove lid.
5. Stir well and serve.

Nutritional Value (Amount per Serving):

- Calories 175
- Fat 4.5 g
- Carbohydrates 29.8 g
- Sugar 0.7 g
- Protein 6.1 g
- Cholesterol 2 mg

Healthy Kidney Bean Dip

Preparation Time: 10 minutes

Cooking Time: 10 minutes

Serve: 2

Ingredients:

- 1 cup dry white kidney beans, soaked overnight and drained
- 1 tbsp fresh lemon juice
- 2 tbsp water
- 1/2 cup coconut yogurt
- 1 roasted garlic clove
- 1 tbsp olive oil
- 1/4 tsp cayenne
- 1 tsp dried parsley
- Pepper
- Salt

Directions:

1. Add soaked beans and 1 3/4 cups of water into the instant pot.
2. Seal pot with lid and cook on high for 10 minutes.
3. Once done, allow to release pressure naturally. Remove lid.
4. Drain beans well and transfer them into the food processor.
5. Add remaining ingredients into the food processor and process until smooth.
6. Serve and enjoy.

Nutritional Value (Amount per Serving):

- Calories 136
- Fat 3.2 g
- Carbohydrates 20 g
- Sugar 2.1 g
- Protein 7.7 g
- Cholesterol 0 mg

Balsamic Bell Pepper Salsa

Preparation Time: 10 minutes

Cooking Time: 6 minutes

Serve: 2

Ingredients:

- 2 red bell peppers, chopped and seeds removed
- 1 cup grape tomatoes, halved
- 1/2 tbsp cayenne
- 1 tbsp balsamic vinegar
- 2 cup vegetable broth
- 1/2 cup sour cream
- 1/2 tsp garlic powder
- 1/2 onion, chopped
- Salt

Directions:

1. Add all ingredients except cream into the instant pot and stir well.
2. Seal pot with lid and cook on high for 6 minutes.
3. Once done, release pressure using quick release. Remove lid.
4. Add sour cream and stir well.
5. Blend the salsa mixture using an immersion blender until smooth.
6. Serve and enjoy.

Nutritional Value (Amount per Serving):

- Calories 235
- Fat 14.2 g
- Carbohydrates 19.8 g
- Sugar 10.7 g
- Protein 9.2 g
- Cholesterol 25 mg

Kidney Bean Spread

Preparation Time: 10 minutes
Cooking Time: 18 minutes
Serve: 2

Ingredients:

- 1 lb dry kidney beans, soaked overnight and drained
- 1 tsp garlic, minced
- 2 tbsp olive oil
- 1 tbsp fresh lemon juice
- 1 tbsp paprika
- 4 cups vegetable stock
- 1/2 cup onion, chopped
- Pepper
- Salt

Directions:

1. Add beans and stock into the instant pot.
2. Seal pot with lid and cook on high for 18 minutes.
3. Once done, allow to release pressure naturally. Remove lid.
4. Drain beans well and reserve 1/2 cup stock.
5. Transfer beans, reserve stock, and remaining ingredients into the food processor and process until smooth.
6. Serve and enjoy.

Nutritional Value (Amount per Serving):

- Calories 461
- Fat 8.6 g
- Carbohydrates 73 g
- Sugar 4 g
- Protein 26.4 g
- Cholesterol 0 mg

Chapter 7: Poultry

Perfect Chicken & Rice

Preparation Time: 10 minutes
Cooking Time: 25 minutes
Serve: 2

Ingredients:

- 1 lb chicken breasts, skinless and boneless
- 1 tsp olive oil
- 1 cup onion, diced
- 1 tsp garlic minced
- 4 carrots, peeled and sliced
- 1 tbsp Mediterranean spice mix
- 2 cups brown rice, rinsed
- 2 cups chicken stock
- Pepper
- Salt

Directions:

1. Add oil into the inner pot of instant pot and set the pot on sauté mode.
2. Add garlic and onion and sauté until onion is softened.
3. Add stock, carrot, rice, and Mediterranean spice mix and stir well.
4. Place chicken on top of rice mixture and season with pepper and salt. Do not mix.
5. Seal pot with a lid and select manual and set timer for 20 minutes.
6. Once done, allow to release pressure naturally for 10 minutes then release remaining using quick release. Remove lid.
7. Remove chicken from pot and shred using a fork.
8. Return shredded chicken to the pot and stir well.
9. Serve and enjoy.

Nutritional Value (Amount per Serving):

- Calories 612
- Fat 12.4 g
- Carbohydrates 81.7 g
- Sugar 4.6 g
- Protein 41.1 g
- Cholesterol 101 mg

Moroccan Chicken

Preparation Time: 10 minutes

Cooking Time: 25 minutes

Serve: 2

Ingredients:

- 2 lbs chicken breasts, cut into chunks
- 1/2 tsp cinnamon
- 1 tsp turmeric
- 1/2 tsp ginger
- 1 tsp cumin
- 2 tbsp Dijon mustard
- 1 tbsp molasses
- 1 tbsp honey
- 2 tbsp tomato paste
- 5 garlic cloves, chopped
- 2 onions, cut into quarters
- 2 green bell peppers, cut into strips
- 2 red bell peppers, cut into strips
- 2 cups olives, pitted
- 1 lemon, peeled and sliced
- 2 tbsp olive oil
- Pepper
- Salt

Directions:

1. Add oil into the inner pot of instant pot and set the pot on sauté mode.
2. Add chicken and sauté for 5 minutes.
3. Add remaining ingredients and stir everything well.
4. Seal pot with a lid and select manual and set timer for 20 minutes.
5. Once done, release pressure using quick release. Remove lid.
6. Stir well and serve.

Nutritional Value (Amount per Serving):

- Calories 446
- Fat 21.2 g
- Carbohydrates 18.5 g
- Sugar 9.7 g
- Protein 45.8 g
- Cholesterol 135 mg

Tasty Turkey Chili

Preparation Time: 10 minutes

Cooking Time: 25 minutes

Serve: 2

Ingredients:

- 1 lb cooked turkey, shredded
- 2 cups chicken broth
- 1 tsp tomato paste
- 1 small onion, chopped
- 1 tbsp Italian seasoning
- 1 tsp garlic powder
- 1 tbsp cumin, roasted
- 1 tbsp chili powder
- 2 cups tomatoes, crushed
- 1 tsp garlic, minced
- 14 oz can red beans, drained
- 14 oz can chickpeas, drained
- 1/2 cup corn
- 2 carrots, peeled and chopped
- 1/2 cup celery, chopped
- 1/4 cup edamame
- 2 tbsp olive oil
- Pepper
- Salt

Directions:

1. Add all ingredients into the instant pot and stir everything well.
2. Seal pot with lid and cook on high for 15 minutes.
3. Once done, allow to release pressure naturally. Remove lid.
4. Set pot on sauté mode and cook for 5-10 minutes or until chili thicken.
5. Stir well and serve.

Nutritional Value (Amount per Serving):

- Calories 593
- Fat 18.1 g
- Carbohydrates 56 g
- Sugar 7.3 g
- Protein 50.9 g
- Cholesterol 88 mg

Flavorful Cafe Rio Chicken

Preparation Time: 10 minutes

Cooking Time: 12 minutes

Serve: 2

Ingredients:

- 2 lbs chicken breasts, skinless and boneless
- 1/2 cup chicken stock
- 2 1/2 tbsp ranch seasoning
- 1/2 tbsp ground cumin
- 1/2 tbsp chili powder
- 1/2 tbsp garlic, minced
- 2/3 cup Italian dressing
- Pepper
- Salt

Directions:

1. Add chicken into the instant pot.
2. Mix together remaining ingredients and pour over chicken.
3. Seal pot with a lid and select manual and set timer for 12 minutes.
4. Once done, allow to release pressure naturally for 10 minutes then release remaining using quick release. Remove lid.
5. Shred the chicken using a fork and serve.

Nutritional Value (Amount per Serving):

- Calories 382
- Fat 18.9 g
- Carbohydrates 3.6 g
- Sugar 2.3 g
- Protein 44.1 g
- Cholesterol 152 mg

Pesto Chicken

Preparation Time: 10 minutes

Cooking Time: 5 minutes

Serve: 2

Ingredients:

- 1 lb chicken thighs, skinless and boneless
- 1/4 cup water
- 1 tsp Italian seasoning
- 2 tbsp basil pesto
- 1/4 cup heavy cream
- 1 tbsp garlic, minced
- 1 cup tomatoes, chopped
- 1 cup onion, diced
- Pepper
- Salt

Directions:

1. Add all ingredients except heavy cream into the instant pot and stir well.
2. Seal pot with lid and cook on high for 5 minutes.
3. Once done, allow to release pressure naturally for 10 minutes then release remaining using quick release. Remove lid.
4. Remove chicken from pot.
5. Add heavy cream into the pot and stir well. Using immersion blender blend pot mixture until smooth and creamy.
6. Pour sauce over chicken and serve.

Nutritional Value (Amount per Serving):

- Calories 268
- Fat 11.7 g
- Carbohydrates 5.5 g
- Sugar 2.5 g
- Protein 33.9 g
- Cholesterol 112 mg

One Pot Chicken & Potatoes

Preparation Time: 10 minutes

Cooking Time: 13 minutes

Serve: 2

Ingredients:

- 6 chicken thighs, bone-in, and skin-on
- 1 tsp oregano
- 1 lb potatoes, halved
- 2 tbsp honey
- 1 fresh lemon juice
- 1 tsp garlic, minced
- 1 cup chicken stock
- 1 tsp paprika
- 1/2 tsp allspice
- 2 tbsp olive oil
- Pepper
- Salt

Directions:

1. In a small bowl, mix together 1 tablespoon oil, allspice, paprika, pepper, and salt and rub over chicken.
2. Add remaining oil into the instant pot and set the pot on sauté mode.
3. Add chicken to the pot and sauté until brown, about 5 minutes.
4. Add remaining ingredients and stir everything well.
5. Seal pot with lid and cook on high for 8 minutes.
6. Once done, allow to release pressure naturally for 5 minutes then release remaining using quick release. Remove lid.
7. Stir well and serve.

Nutritional Value (Amount per Serving):

- Calories 397
- Fat 15.8 g
- Carbohydrates 18.6 g
- Sugar 7 g
- Protein 43.8 g
- Cholesterol 130 mg

Delicious Gyro Chicken

Preparation Time: 10 minutes
Cooking Time: 12 minutes
Serve: 2

Ingredients:

- 1 lb chicken thighs
- 1 cup chicken broth
- 1 tsp garlic, minced
- 1 tbsp fresh lemon juice
- 1 tbsp olive oil
- 2 tbsp fresh cilantro, chopped
- 1 tbsp green onion, chopped
- 1/2 tsp oregano
- 1/2 tsp cumin powder
- 1/2 tsp ground cinnamon
- 1/2 tsp paprika
- 1/2 tsp Adobo seasoning
- 1 onion, sliced
- Pepper
- Salt

Directions:

1. Season chicken with oregano, cinnamon, cumin, paprika, adobo seasoning, pepper, and salt and place into the instant pot.
2. Pour remaining ingredients over chicken.
3. Seal pot with lid and cook on high for 12 minutes.
4. Once done, release pressure using quick release. Remove lid.
5. Stir well and serve.

Nutritional Value (Amount per Serving):

- Calories 362
- Fat 16.6 g
- Carbohydrates 5.2 g
- Sugar 2 g
- Protein 46.1 g
- Cholesterol 135 mg

Flavorful Mediterranean Chicken

Preparation Time: 10 minutes

Cooking Time: 20 minutes

Serve: 2

Ingredients:

- 2 lbs chicken thighs
- 1/2 cup olives
- 28 oz can tomato, diced
- 1 1/2 tsp dried oregano
- 2 tsp dried parsley
- 1/2 tsp ground coriander powder
- 1/4 tsp chili pepper
- 1 tsp onion powder
- 1 sp paprika
- 2 cups onion, chopped
- 2 tbsp olive oil
- Pepper
- Salt

Directions:

1. Add oil into the inner pot of instant pot and set the pot on sauté mode.
2. Add chicken and cook until browned. Transfer chicken on a plate.
3. Add onion and sauté for 5 minutes.
4. Add all spices, tomatoes, and salt and cook for 2-3 minutes.
5. Return chicken to the pot and stir everything well.
6. Seal pot with lid and cook on high for 8 minutes.
7. Once done, release pressure using quick release. Remove lid.
8. Add olives and stir well.
9. Serve and enjoy.

Nutritional Value (Amount per Serving):

- Calories 292
- Fat 13 g
- Carbohydrates 8.9 g
- Sugar 4.8 g
- Protein 34.3 g
- Cholesterol 101 mg

Chapter 8: Beef

Tasty Beef Stew

Preparation Time: 10 minutes
Cooking Time: 30 minutes
Serve: 2

Ingredients:

- 2 1/2 lbs beef roast, cut into chunks
- 1 cup beef broth
- 1/2 cup balsamic vinegar
- 1 tbsp honey
- 1/2 tsp red pepper flakes
- 1 tbsp garlic, minced
- Pepper
- Salt

Directions:

1. Add all ingredients into the inner pot of instant pot and stir well.
2. Seal pot with lid and cook on high for 30 minutes.
3. Once done, allow to release pressure naturally. Remove lid.
4. Stir well and serve.

Nutritional Value (Amount per Serving):

- Calories 562
- Fat 18.1 g
- Carbohydrates 5.7 g
- Sugar 4.6 g
- Protein 87.4 g
- Cholesterol 253 mg

Italian Beef Roast

Preparation Time: 10 minutes

Cooking Time: 50 minutes

Serve: 2

Ingredients:

- 2 1/2 lbs beef roast, cut into chunks
- 1 cup chicken broth
- 1 cup red wine
- 2 tbsp Italian seasoning
- 2 tbsp olive oil
- 1 bell pepper, chopped
- 2 celery stalks, chopped
- 1 tsp garlic, minced
- 1 onion, sliced
- Pepper
- Salt

Directions:

1. Add oil into the instant pot and set the pot on sauté mode.
2. Add the meat into the pot and sauté until brown.
3. Add onion, bell pepper, and celery and sauté for 5 minutes.
4. Add remaining ingredients and stir well.
5. Seal pot with lid and cook on high for 40 minutes.
6. Once done, allow to release pressure naturally. Remove lid.
7. Stir well and serve.

Nutritional Value (Amount per Serving):

- Calories 460
- Fat 18.2 g
- Carbohydrates 5.3 g
- Sugar 2.7 g
- Protein 58.7 g
- Cholesterol 172 mg

Beef Curry

Preparation Time: 10 minutes

Cooking Time: 30 minutes

Serve: 2

Ingredients:

- 1/2 lb beef stew meat, cubed
- 1 bell peppers, sliced
- 1 cup beef stock
- 1 tbsp fresh ginger, grated
- 1/2 tsp ground cumin
- 1 tsp ground coriander
- 1/2 tsp cayenne pepper
- 1/2 cup sun-roasted tomatoes, diced
- 2 tbsp olive oil
- 1 tsp garlic, crushed
- 1 green chili peppers, chopped

Directions:

1. Add all ingredients into the instant pot and stir well.
2. Seal pot with lid and cook on high for 30 minutes.
3. Once done, allow to release pressure naturally. Remove lid.
4. Serve and enjoy.

Nutritional Value (Amount per Serving):

- Calories 391
- Fat 21.9 g
- Carbohydrates 11.6 g
- Sugar 5.8 g
- Protein 37.4 g
- Cholesterol 101 mg

Jalapeno Beef Chili

Preparation Time: 10 minutes

Cooking Time: 40 minutes

Serve: 2

Ingredients:

- 1 lb ground beef
- 1 tsp garlic powder
- 1 jalapeno pepper, chopped
- 1 tbsp ground cumin
- 1 tbsp chili powder
- 1 lb ground pork
- 4 tomatillos, chopped
- 1/2 onion, chopped
- 5 oz tomato paste
- Pepper
- Salt

Directions:

1. Add oil into the instant pot and set the pot on sauté mode.
2. Add beef and pork and cook until brown.
3. Add remaining ingredients and stir well.
4. Seal pot with lid and cook on high for 35 minutes.
5. Once done, allow to release pressure naturally. Remove lid.
6. Stir well and serve.

Nutritional Value (Amount per Serving):

- Calories 217
- Fat 6.1 g
- Carbohydrates 6.2 g
- Sugar 2.7 g
- Protein 33.4 g
- Cholesterol 92 mg

Italian Beef

Preparation Time: 10 minutes
Cooking Time: 35 minutes
Serve: 2

Ingredients:

- 1 lb ground beef
- 1 tbsp olive oil
- 1/2 cup mozzarella cheese, shredded
- 1/2 cup tomato puree
- 1 tsp basil
- 1 tsp oregano
- 1/2 onion, chopped
- 1 carrot, chopped
- 14 oz can tomatoes, diced
- Pepper
- Salt

Directions:

1. Add oil into the instant pot and set the pot on sauté mode.
2. Add onion and sauté for 2 minutes.
3. Add meat and sauté until browned.
4. Add remaining ingredients except for cheese and stir well.
5. Seal pot with lid and cook on high for 35 minutes.
6. Once done, release pressure using quick release. Remove lid.
7. Add cheese and stir well and cook on sauté mode until cheese is melted.
8. Serve and enjoy.

Nutritional Value (Amount per Serving):

- Calories 297
- Fat 11.3 g
- Carbohydrates 11.1 g
- Sugar 6.2 g
- Protein 37.1 g
- Cholesterol 103 mg

Cauliflower Tomato Beef

Preparation Time: 10 minutes

Cooking Time: 25 minutes

Serve: 2

Ingredients:

- 1/2 lb beef stew meat, chopped
- 1 tsp paprika
- 1 tbsp balsamic vinegar
- 1 celery stalk, chopped
- 1/4 cup grape tomatoes, chopped
- 1 onion, chopped
- 1 tbsp olive oil
- 1/4 cup cauliflower, chopped
- Pepper
- Salt

Directions:

1. Add oil into the instant pot and set the pot on sauté mode.
2. Add meat and sauté for 5 minutes.
3. Add remaining ingredients and stir well.
4. Seal pot with lid and cook on high for 20 minutes.
5. Once done, allow to release pressure naturally. Remove lid.
6. Stir and serve.

Nutritional Value (Amount per Serving):

- Calories 306
- Fat 14.3 g
- Carbohydrates 7.6 g
- Sugar 3.5 g
- Protein 35.7 g
- Cholesterol 101 mg

Lemon Basil Beef

Preparation Time: 10 minutes

Cooking Time: 35 minutes

Serve: 2

Ingredients:

- 1 1/2 lb beef stew meat, cut into cubes
- 1/2 cup fresh basil, chopped
- 1/2 tsp dried thyme
- 2 cups chicken stock
- 1 tsp garlic, minced
- 2 tbsp lemon juice
- 1 onion, chopped
- 2 tbsp olive oil
- Pepper
- Salt

Directions:

1. Add oil into the instant pot and set the pot on sauté mode.
2. Add meat, garlic, and onion and sauté for 5 minutes.
3. Add remaining ingredients and stir well.
4. Seal pot with lid and cook on high for 30 minutes.
5. Once done, allow to release pressure naturally. Remove lid.
6. Serve and enjoy.

Nutritional Value (Amount per Serving):

- Calories 396
- Fat 18 g
- Carbohydrates 3.5 g
- Sugar 1.7 g
- Protein 52.4 g
- Cholesterol 152 mg

Sage Tomato Beef

Preparation Time: 10 minutes
Cooking Time: 40 minutes
Serve: 2

Ingredients:

- 2 lbs beef stew meat, cubed
- 1/4 cup tomato paste
- 1 tsp garlic, minced
- 2 cups chicken stock
- 1 onion, chopped
- 2 tbsp olive oil
- 1 tbsp sage, chopped
- Pepper
- Salt

Directions:

1. Add oil into the instant pot and set the pot on sauté mode.
2. Add garlic and onion and sauté for 5 minutes.
3. Add meat and sauté for 5 minutes.
4. Add remaining ingredients and stir well.
5. Seal pot with lid and cook on high for 30 minutes.
6. Once done, allow to release pressure naturally. Remove lid.
7. Serve and enjoy.

Nutritional Value (Amount per Serving):

- Calories 515
- Fat 21.5 g
- Carbohydrates 7 g
- Sugar 3.6 g
- Protein 70 g
- Cholesterol 203 mg

Chapter 9: Pork

Lime Salsa Pork Chops

Preparation Time: 10 minutes

Cooking Time: 25 minutes

Serve: 2

Ingredients:

- 1 1/2 lbs pork chops
- 1/2 tsp garlic powder
- 1/2 tsp ground cumin
- 2 tbsp lime juice
- 1/2 cup salsa
- 1 tbsp olive oil
- Pepper
- Salt

Directions:

1. Add oil into the inner pot of instant pot and set the pot on sauté mode.
2. Add pork chops and sauté until brown.
3. Add remaining ingredients and stir well.
4. Seal pot with lid and cook on high for 15 minutes.
5. Once done, release pressure using quick release. Remove lid.
6. Serve and enjoy.

Nutritional Value (Amount per Serving):

- Calories 591
- Fat 45.9 g
- Carbohydrates 4.3 g
- Sugar 1.5 g
- Protein 38.9 g
- Cholesterol 146 mg

Basil Pork Broccoli

Preparation Time: 10 minutes

Cooking Time: 30 minutes

Serve: 2

Ingredients:

- 1 1/2 lbs pork stew meat, cut into cubes
- 1 tbsp basil, chopped
- 1 1/2 cup chicken stock
- 1/4 cup can tomato, crushed
- 1 cup parmesan cheese, grated
- 2 cups broccoli florets
- 1 tbsp olive oil
- Pepper
- Salt

Directions:

1. Add oil into the inner pot of instant pot and set the pot on sauté mode.
2. Add meat and sauté for 5 minutes.
3. Add remaining ingredients except for cheese and stir well.
4. Seal pot with lid and cook on high for 25 minutes.
5. Once done, release pressure using quick release. Remove lid.
6. Sprinkle with cheese and serve.

Nutritional Value (Amount per Serving):

- Calories 484
- Fat 25.1 g
- Carbohydrates 4.6 g
- Sugar 1 g
- Protein 58.7 g
- Cholesterol 162 mg

Delicious Pork Roast

Preparation Time: 10 minutes

Cooking Time: 35 minutes

Serve: 2

Ingredients:

- 1 1/2 lbs pork roast
- 1 cup chicken stock
- 1 tbsp balsamic vinegar
- 1 tbsp olive oil
- 1 tsp dried oregano
- 2 tbsp chili powder
- 1 tbsp garlic, minced
- 14 oz can tomatoes, crushed
- 1 onion, chopped
- Pepper
- Salt

Directions:

1. Add oil into the inner pot of instant pot and set the pot on sauté mode.
2. Add garlic and onion and sauté for 5 minutes.
3. Add remaining ingredients and stir well.
4. Seal pot with lid and cook on high for 30 minutes.
5. Once done, allow to release pressure naturally. Remove lid.
6. Serve and enjoy.

Nutritional Value (Amount per Serving):

- Calories 436
- Fat 20.7 g
- Carbohydrates 10.7 g
- Sugar 5.2 g
- Protein 50.4 g
- Cholesterol 146 mg

Simple Paprika Pork Chops

Preparation Time: 10 minutes

Cooking Time: 25 minutes

Serve: 2

Ingredients:

- 4 pork chops
- 1 tbsp paprika
- 1/4 cup can tomato, crushed
- 2 tbsp olive oil
- 1/2 tsp chili powder
- 1 onion, chopped
- 1 cup chicken stock
- Pepper
- Salt

Directions:

1. Add oil into the inner pot of instant pot and set the pot on sauté mode.
2. Add pork chops sauté for 5 minutes.
3. Add remaining ingredients stir well.
4. Seal pot with lid and cook on high for 20 minutes.
5. Once done, allow to release pressure naturally for 10 minutes then release remaining using quick release. Remove lid.
6. Serve and enjoy.

Nutritional Value (Amount per Serving):

- Calories 338
- Fat 27.4 g
- Carbohydrates 4.4 g
- Sugar 1.6 g
- Protein 18.9 g
- Cholesterol 69 mg

Simple Lemon Pepper Pork Chops

Preparation Time: 10 minutes

Cooking Time: 15 minutes

Serve: 2

Ingredients:

- 1/2 lb pork chops
- 1 1/2 tbsp lemon pepper seasoning
- 1/4 cup chicken stock
- Salt

Directions:

1. Season pork chops with lemon pepper seasoning and salt.
2. Set pot on sauté mode.
3. Add pork chops and sauté until brown. Pour stock over pork chops.
4. Seal pot with lid and cook on high for 10 minutes.
5. Once done, release pressure using quick release. Remove lid.
6. Serve and enjoy.

Nutritional Value (Amount per Serving):

- Calories 376
- Fat 28.4 g
- Carbohydrates 3.2 g
- Sugar 0.1 g
- Protein 26.1 g
- Cholesterol 98 mg

Garlic Parsley Pork Chops

Preparation Time: 10 minutes

Cooking Time: 25 minutes

Serve: 2

Ingredients:

- 4 pork chops, boneless
- 1 tbsp garlic, minced
- 1/2 cup tomato puree
- 1 cup chicken stock
- 1 onion, chopped
- 1 tbsp fresh parsley, chopped
- 1 tbsp olive oil
- Pepper
- Salt

Directions:

1. Add oil into the inner pot of instant pot and set the pot on sauté mode.
2. Add garlic and onion and sauté for 2 minutes.
3. Add pork chops and sauté for 3 minutes.
4. Add remaining ingredients and stir well.
5. Seal pot with lid and cook on high for 20 minutes.
6. Once done, allow to release pressure naturally for 10 minutes then release remaining using quick release. Remove lid.
7. Stir and serve.

Nutritional Value (Amount per Serving):

- Calories 315
- Fat 23.6 g
- Carbohydrates 6.3 g
- Sugar 2.9 g
- Protein 19.1 g
- Cholesterol 69 mg

Pork with Carrots Potatoes

Preparation Time: 10 minutes

Cooking Time: 15 minutes

Serve: 2

Ingredients:

- 2 pork chops, boneless
- 1/4 cup balsamic vinegar
- 2 tbsp honey
- 1 1/2 tsp ground ginger
- 1 tsp curry powder
- 1/2 cup chicken stock
- 1 tbsp olive oil
- 3 carrots, chopped
- 3 small potatoes, cubed
- 2 garlic cloves, chopped
- Pepper
- Salt

Directions:

1. Add oil into the instant pot and set the pot on sauté mode.
2. Add pork chops into the pot and brown them from both the sides.
3. Add remaining ingredients to the pot and stir well.
4. Seal pot with lid and cook on high for 10 minutes.
5. Once done, allow to release pressure naturally. Open the lid.
6. Serve and enjoy.

Nutritional Value (Amount per Serving):

- Calories 615
- Fat 27.5 g
- Carbohydrates 69.4 g
- Sugar 25.1 g
- Protein 23.7 g
- Cholesterol 69 mg

Tasty Pork Carnitas

Preparation Time: 10 minutes

Cooking Time: 35 minutes

Serve: 2

Ingredients:

- 1 lb pork shoulder
- 1/4 cup of water
- 1 cup chicken broth
- 1/2 tbsp olive oil
- 1 tsp garlic, minced
- 1/2 tsp cumin
- 1/2 tsp oregano
- 1/2 onion, chopped
- 1 lime juice
- Pepper
- Salt

Directions:

1. Add oil into the instant pot and set the pot on sauté mode.
2. Add meat to the pot and sauté until browned.
3. Add remaining ingredients and stir well.
4. Seal pot with lid and cook on high for 30 minutes.
5. Once done, allow to release pressure naturally. Open the lid.
6. Remove meat from pot and shred using a fork and serve.

Nutritional Value (Amount per Serving):

- Calories 367
- Fat 26.5 g
- Carbohydrates 2.9 g
- Sugar 1 g
- Protein 27.9 g
- Cholesterol 102 mg

Chapter 10: Lamb

Delicious Salsa Lamb

Preparation Time: 10 minutes

Cooking Time: 35 minutes

Serve: 2

Ingredients:

- 1 lb lamb shoulder, cut into chunks
- 1/4 cup fresh cilantro, chopped
- 2 tbsp olive oil
- 1 onion, chopped
- 1 tsp garlic, minced
- 1 1/2 cups salsa
- Pepper
- Salt

Directions:

1. Add oil into the inner pot of instant pot and set the pot on sauté mode.
2. Add garlic and onion and sauté for 5 minutes.
3. Add remaining ingredients and stir well.
4. Seal pot with lid and cook on high for 30 minutes.
5. Once done, allow to release pressure naturally. Remove lid.
6. Stir well and serve.

Nutritional Value (Amount per Serving):

- Calories 310
- Fat 15.5 g
- Carbohydrates 9 g
- Sugar 4.2 g
- Protein 33.7 g
- Cholesterol 102 mg

Flavors Lamb Ribs

Preparation Time: 10 minutes

Cooking Time: 25 minutes

Serve: 2

Ingredients:

- 4 lamb ribs
- 2 tomatoes, chopped
- 2 tbsp olive oil
- 1 1/2 cups chicken stock
- 1 tbsp sage, chopped
- 1 tbsp garlic, minced
- Pepper
- Salt

Directions:

1. Add oil into the inner pot of instant pot and set the pot on sauté mode.
2. Add lamb ribs and sear for 5 minutes.
3. Add remaining ingredients except for heavy cream and stir well.
4. Seal pot with lid and cook on high for 20 minutes.
5. Once done, allow to release pressure naturally for 10 minutes then release remaining using quick release. Remove lid.
6. Serve and enjoy.

Nutritional Value (Amount per Serving):

- Calories 539
- Fat 46.1 g
- Carbohydrates 10.9 g
- Sugar 7.2 g
- Protein 22.6 g
- Cholesterol 0 mg

Herb Veggie Lamb

Preparation Time: 10 minutes

Cooking Time: 30 minutes

Serve: 2

Ingredients:

- 1 1/2 lbs lamb stew meat, cubed
- 1 tbsp cilantro, chopped
- 1 cup tomato puree
- 1 eggplant, chopped
- 1 tomato, chopped
- 1 carrot, chopped
- 1 zucchini, chopped
- 1 cup beef stock
- 1 tbsp tarragon, chopped
- 1 onion, chopped
- Pepper
- Salt

Directions:

1. Add oil into the inner pot of instant pot and set the pot on sauté mode.
2. Add meat and onion and sauté for 5 minutes.
3. Add remaining ingredients and stir well.
4. Seal pot with lid and cook on high for 25 minutes.
5. Once done, allow to release pressure naturally. Remove lid.
6. Serve and enjoy.

Nutritional Value (Amount per Serving):

- Calories 405
- Fat 13.2 g
- Carbohydrates 19.5 g
- Sugar 10 g
- Protein 52 g
- Cholesterol 153 mg

Garlic Mushrooms Lamb Chops

Preparation Time: 10 minutes

Cooking Time: 15 minutes

Serve: 2

Ingredients:

- 1 lb lamb chops
- 2 cups beef stock
- 1 cup mushrooms, sliced
- 2 tbsp olive oil
- 1 tsp garlic, minced
- Pepper
- Salt

Directions:

1. Add all ingredients into the inner pot of instant pot and stir well.
2. Seal pot with lid and cook on high for 15 minutes.
3. Once done, release pressure using quick release. Remove lid.
4. Stir and serve.

Nutritional Value (Amount per Serving):

- Calories 284
- Fat 15.6 g
- Carbohydrates 0.9 g
- Sugar 0.3 g
- Protein 33.8 g
- Cholesterol 102 mg

Tasty Lamb Leg

Preparation Time: 10 minutes

Cooking Time: 20 minutes

Serve: 2

Ingredients:

- 2 lbs leg of lamb, boneless and cut into chunks
- 1 tbsp olive oil
- 1 tbsp garlic, sliced
- 1 cup red wine
- 1 cup onion, chopped
- 2 carrots, chopped
- 1 tsp rosemary, chopped
- 2 tsp thyme, chopped
- 1 tsp oregano, chopped
- 1/2 cup beef stock
- 2 tbsp tomato paste
- Pepper
- Salt

Directions:

1. Add oil into the inner pot of instant pot and set the pot on sauté mode.
2. Add meat and sauté until browned.
3. Add remaining ingredients and stir well.
4. Seal pot with lid and cook on high for 15 minutes.
5. Once done, allow to release pressure naturally. Remove lid.
6. Stir well and serve.

Nutritional Value (Amount per Serving):

- Calories 540
- Fat 20.4 g
- Carbohydrates 10.3 g
- Sugar 4.2 g
- Protein 65.2 g
- Cholesterol 204 mg

Healthy Lamb & Couscous

Preparation Time: 10 minutes

Cooking Time: 43 minutes

Serve: 2

Ingredients:

- 4 lamb chops
- 2 celery stalks, chopped
- 1 tbsp olive oil
- 1 tbsp basil, chopped
- 1 tbsp oregano, chopped
- 1 tbsp almonds, chopped
- 3 cups beef stock
- 1 1/2 cusp couscous
- Pepper
- Salt

Directions:

1. Add oil into the inner pot of instant pot and set the pot on sauté mode.
2. Add the meat into the pot and sauté for 3 minutes.
3. Add the rest of the ingredients and stir well.
4. Seal pot with lid and cook on low pressure for 40 minutes.
5. Once done, allow to release pressure naturally. Remove lid.
6. Serve and enjoy.

Nutritional Value (Amount per Serving):

- Calories 908
- Fat 29.2 g
- Carbohydrates 51.7 g
- Sugar 0.2 g
- Protein 102.7 g
- Cholesterol 294 mg

Curried Lamb Stew

Preparation Time: 10 minutes
Cooking Time: 20 minutes
Serve: 2

Ingredients:
- 1 lb lamb shoulder, cut into cubes
- 1/4 cup heavy cream
- 2 cups beef stock
- 1 tbsp basil, chopped
- 1 tsp chili powder
- 1/2 tbsp curry powder
- 1 onion, chopped
- 1 tbsp olive oil
- Pepper
- Salt

Directions:
1. Add oil into the inner pot of instant pot and set the pot on sauté mode.
2. Add onion and sauté for 5 minutes.
3. Add meat and sauté for 5 minutes.
4. Add the rest of ingredients except cream and stir well.
5. Seal pot with lid and cook on high for 10 minutes.
6. Once done, release pressure using quick release. Remove lid.
7. Stir in cream and serve.

Nutritional Value (Amount per Serving):
- Calories 291
- Fat 15.1 g
- Carbohydrates 3.7 g
- Sugar 1.3 g
- Protein 33.9 g
- Cholesterol 112 mg

Lamb with Beans

Preparation Time: 10 minutes

Cooking Time: 35 minutes

Serve: 2

Ingredients:

- 2 lbs lamb meat, cut into chunks
- 1/4 cup cilantro, chopped
- 1 tbsp garlic, minced
- 1/4 cup can tomato, crushed
- 1 cup beef stock
- 2 cups can red beans, rinsed and drained
- 1 onion, chopped
- 2 tbsp olive oil
- Pepper
- Salt

Directions:

1. Add oil into the inner pot of instant pot and set the pot on sauté mode.
2. Add garlic, onion, and meat and sauté for 5 minutes.
3. Add the rest of the ingredients and stir well.
4. Seal pot with lid and cook on high for 30 minutes.
5. Once done, allow to release pressure naturally. Remove lid.
6. Serve and enjoy.

Nutritional Value (Amount per Serving):

- Calories 650
- Fat 37.8 g
- Carbohydrates 23.7 g
- Sugar 3.6 g
- Protein 50.1 g
- Cholesterol 161 mg

Chapter 11: Seafood & Fish

Shrimp Scampi

Preparation Time: 10 minutes

Cooking Time: 8 minutes

Serve: 2

Ingredients:

- 1 lb whole wheat penne pasta
- 1 lb frozen shrimp
- 2 tbsp garlic, minced
- 1/4 tsp cayenne
- 1/2 tbsp Italian seasoning
- 1/4 cup olive oil
- 3 1/2 cups fish stock
- Pepper
- Salt

Directions:

1. Add all ingredients into the inner pot of instant pot and stir well.
2. Seal pot with lid and cook on high for 6 minutes.
3. Once done, release pressure using quick release. Remove lid.
4. Stir well and serve.

Nutritional Value (Amount per Serving):

- Calories 435
- Fat 12.6 g
- Carbohydrates 54.9 g
- Sugar 0.1 g
- Protein 30.6 g
- Cholesterol 116 mg

Basil Fish Curry

Preparation Time: 10 minutes

Cooking Time: 8 minutes

Serve: 2

Ingredients:

- 10 oz tilapia fillets, chopped
- 1/2 tsp turmeric
- 1 tsp ground cumin
- 1 1/2 tsp chili powder
- 1 tsp ground coriander
- 1/2 cup fresh basil, chopped
- 1 tsp fresh lemon juice
- 3 tbsp olive oil
- 1 chili pepper, chopped
- 1/2 cup grape tomatoes, chopped
- 2 cups of coconut milk
- 1 tsp garlic, minced
- 1 small onion, chopped
- Salt

Directions:

1. Add oil into the inner pot of instant pot and set the pot on sauté mode.
2. Add garlic, onion, salt, and all spices and cook for 2-4 minutes.
3. Add coconut milk and stir well.
4. Add chili pepper, fish, and grape tomatoes and stir well.
5. Seal pot with lid and cook on high for 4 minutes.
6. Once done, release pressure using quick release. Remove lid.
7. Stir in basil and serve.

Nutritional Value (Amount per Serving):

- Calories 444
- Fat 40.2 g
- Carbohydrates 10.5 g
- Sugar 5.5 g
- Protein 16.7 g
- Cholesterol 35 mg

Crab Stew

Preparation Time: 10 minutes
Cooking Time: 13 minutes
Serve: 2

Ingredients:

- 1/2 lb lump crab meat
- 2 tbsp heavy cream
- 1 tbsp olive oil
- 2 cups fish stock
- 1/2 lb shrimp, shelled and chopped
- 1 celery stalk, chopped
- 1/2 tsp garlic, chopped
- 1/4 onion, chopped
- Pepper
- Salt

Directions:

1. Add oil into the inner pot of instant pot and set the pot on sauté mode.
2. Add onion and sauté for 3 minutes.
3. Add garlic and sauté for 30 seconds.
4. Add remaining ingredients except for heavy cream and stir well.
5. Seal pot with lid and cook on high for 10 minutes.
6. Once done, release pressure using quick release. Remove lid.
7. Stir in heavy cream and serve.

Nutritional Value (Amount per Serving):

- Calories 376
- Fat 25.5 g
- Carbohydrates 5.8 g
- Sugar 0.7 g
- Protein 48.1 g
- Cholesterol 326 mg

Quick & Easy Shrimp

Preparation Time: 10 minutes

Cooking Time: 1 minute

Serve: 2

Directions:

- 1 3/4 lbs shrimp, frozen and deveined
- 1/2 cup fish stock
- 1/2 cup apple cider vinegar
- Pepper
- Salt

Directions:

1. Add all ingredients into the inner pot of instant pot and stir well.
2. Seal pot with lid and cook on high for 1 minute.
3. Once done, release pressure using quick release. Remove lid.
4. Stir and serve.

Nutritional Value (Amount per Serving):

- Calories 165
- Fat 2.4 g
- Carbohydrates 2.2 g
- Sugar 0.1 g
- Protein 30.6 g
- Cholesterol 279 mg

Dijon Fish Fillets

Preparation Time: 10 minutes

Cooking Time: 3 minutes

Serve: 2

Ingredients:

- 2 white fish fillets
- 1 tbsp Dijon mustard
- 1 cup of water
- Pepper
- Salt

Directions:

1. Pour water into the instant pot and place trivet in the pot.
2. Brush fish fillets with mustard and season with pepper and salt and place on top of the trivet.
3. Seal pot with lid and cook on high for 3 minutes.
4. Once done, release pressure using quick release. Remove lid.
5. Serve and enjoy.

Nutritional Value (Amount per Serving):

- Calories 270
- Fat 11.9 g
- Carbohydrates 0.5 g
- Sugar 0.1 g
- Protein 38 g
- Cholesterol 119 mg

Delicious Lemon Butter Cod

Preparation Time: 10 minutes

Cooking Time: 8 minutes

Serve: 2

Ingredients:

- 1 1/2 lbs fresh cod fillets
- 28 oz can tomato, diced
- 1 tsp oregano
- 1 onion, sliced
- 1 lemon juice
- 3 tbsp butter
- Pepper
- Salt

Directions:

1. Add butter into the instant pot and set the pot on sauté mode.
2. Add onion and sauté for 5 minutes.
3. Add remaining ingredients and stir everything well.
4. Seal pot with lid and cook on high for 3 minutes.
5. Once done, release pressure using quick release. Remove lid.
6. Stir well and serve.

Nutritional Value (Amount per Serving):

- Calories 231
- Fat 6.9 g
- Carbohydrates 29 g
- Sugar 7.5 g
- Protein 14.7 g
- Cholesterol 51 mg

Lemoney Prawns

Preparation Time: 10 minutes

Cooking Time: 3 minutes

Serve: 2

Ingredients:

- 1/2 lb prawns
- 1/2 cup fish stock
- 1 tbsp fresh lemon juice
- 1 tbsp lemon zest, grated
- 1 tbsp olive oil
- 1 tbsp garlic, minced
- Pepper
- Salt

Directions:

1. Add all ingredients into the inner pot of instant pot and stir well.
2. Seal pot with lid and cook on high for 3 minutes.
3. Once done, release pressure using quick release. Remove lid.
4. Drain prawns and serve.

Nutritional Value (Amount per Serving):

- Calories 215
- Fat 9.5 g
- Carbohydrates 3.9 g
- Sugar 0.4 g
- Protein 27.6 g
- Cholesterol 239 mg

Lemon Cod Peas

Preparation Time: 10 minutes

Cooking Time: 10 minutes

Serve: 2

Ingredients:

- 1 lb cod fillets, skinless, boneless and cut into chunks
- 1 cup fish stock
- 1 tbsp fresh parsley, chopped
- 1/2 tbsp lemon juice
- 1 green chili, chopped
- 3/4 cup fresh peas
- 2 tbsp onion, chopped
- Pepper
- Salt

Directions:

1. Add all ingredients into the inner pot of instant pot and stir well.
2. Seal pot with lid and cook on high for 10 minutes.
3. Once done, release pressure using quick release. Remove lid.
4. Stir and serve.

Nutritional Value (Amount per Serving):

- Calories 128
- Fat 1.6 g
- Carbohydrates 5 g
- Sugar 2.1 g
- Protein 23.2 g
- Cholesterol 41 mg

Chapter 12: Desserts

Delicious Apple Pear Cobbler

Preparation Time: 10 minutes

Cooking Time: 12 minutes

Serve: 2

Ingredients:

- 3 apples, cored and cut into chunks
- 1 cup steel-cut oats
- 2 pears, cored and cut into chunks
- 1/4 cup maple syrup
- 1 1/2 cups water
- 1 tsp cinnamon

Directions:

1. Spray instant pot from inside with cooking spray.
2. Add all ingredients into the inner pot of instant pot and stir well.
3. Seal pot with lid and cook on high for 12 minutes.
4. Once done, release pressure using quick release. Remove lid.
5. Sere and enjoy.

Nutritional Value (Amount per Serving):

- Calories 278
- Fat 1.8 g
- Carbohydrates 66.5 g
- Sugar 39.5 g
- Protein 3.5 g
- Cholesterol 0 mg

Applesauce

Preparation Time: 10 minutes

Cooking Time: 1 minute

Serve: 2

Ingredients:

- 3 lbs apples, peeled, cored, and diced
- 1/3 cup apple juice
- 1/2 tsp ground cinnamon

Directions:

1. Add all ingredients into the instant pot and stir well.
2. Seal pot with lid and cook on high for 1 minute.
3. Once done, allow to release pressure naturally. Remove lid.
4. Blend apple mixture using an immersion blender until smooth.
5. Serve and enjoy.

Nutritional Value (Amount per Serving):

- Calories 32
- Fat 0.1 g
- Carbohydrates 8.6 g
- Sugar 6.5 g
- Protein 0.2 g
- Cholesterol 0 mg

Lime Pears

Preparation Time: 10 minutes

Cooking Time: 10 minutes

Serve: 2

Ingredients:

- 4 pears, cored & cut into wedges
- 1/2 tsp vanilla
- 1 cup apple juice
- 1 tsp lime zest, grated
- 1 lime juice

Directions:

1. Add all ingredients into the inner pot of instant pot and stir well.
2. Seal pot with lid and cook on high for 10 minutes.
3. Once done, allow to release pressure naturally for 10 minutes then release remaining using quick release. Remove lid.
4. Stir and serve.

Nutritional Value (Amount per Serving):

- Calories 151
- Fat 0.4 g
- Carbohydrates 39.9 g
- Sugar 26.7 g
- Protein 0.9 g
- Cholesterol 0 mg

Sweet Pear Stew

Preparation Time: 10 minutes

Cooking Time: 15 minutes

Serve: 2

Ingredients:

- 4 pears, cored and cut into wedges
- 1 tsp vanilla
- 1/4 cup apple juice
- 2 cups grapes, halved

Directions:

1. Add all ingredients into the inner pot of instant pot and stir well.
2. Seal pot with lid and cook on high for 15 minutes.
3. Once done, allow to release pressure naturally for 10 minutes then release remaining using quick release. Remove lid.
4. Stir and serve.

Nutritional Value (Amount per Serving):

- Calories 162
- Fat 0.5 g
- Carbohydrates 41.6 g
- Sugar 29.5 g
- Protein 1.1 g
- Cholesterol 0 mg

Vanilla Apple Compote

Preparation Time: 10 minutes

Cooking Time: 15 minutes

Serve: 2

Ingredients:

- 3 cups apples, cored and cubed
- 1 tsp vanilla
- 3/4 cup coconut sugar
- 1 cup of water
- 2 tbsp fresh lime juice

Directions:

1. Add all ingredients into the inner pot of instant pot and stir well.
2. Seal pot with lid and cook on high for 15 minutes.
3. Once done, allow to release pressure naturally for 10 minutes then release remaining using quick release. Remove lid.
4. Stir and serve.

Nutritional Value (Amount per Serving):

- Calories 76
- Fat 0.2 g
- Carbohydrates 19.1 g
- Sugar 11.9 g
- Protein 0.5 g
- Cholesterol 0 mg

Blackberry Jam

Preparation Time: 10 minutes

Cooking Time: 6 hours

Serve: 2

Ingredients:

- 3 cups fresh blackberries
- 1/4 cup chia seeds
- 4 tbsp Swerve
- 1/4 cup fresh lemon juice
- 1/4 cup coconut butter

Directions:

1. Add all ingredients into the instant pot and stir well.
2. Seal the pot with a lid and select slow cook mode and cook on low for 6 hours.
3. Pour in container and store in fridge.

Nutritional Value (Amount per Serving):

- Calories 101
- Fat 6.8 g
- Carbohydrates 20 g
- Sugar 14.4 g
- Protein 2 g
- Cholesterol 0 mg

Chocolate Nut Spread

Preparation Time: 10 minutes

Cooking Time: 10 minutes

Serve: 2

Ingredients:

- 1/4 cup unsweetened cocoa powder
- 1/4 tsp nutmeg
- 1 tsp vanilla
- 1/4 cup coconut oil
- 1 tsp liquid stevia
- 1/4 cup coconut cream
- 3 tbsp walnuts
- 1 cup almonds

Directions:

1. Add walnut and almonds into the food processor and process until smooth.
2. Add oil and process for 1 minute. Transfer to the bowl and stir in vanilla, nutmeg, and liquid stevia.
3. Add coconut cream into the instant pot and set the pot on sauté mode.
4. Add almond mixture and cocoa powder and stir well and cook for 5 minutes.
5. Pour into the container and store it in the refrigerator for 30 minutes.
6. Serve and enjoy.

Nutritional Value (Amount per Serving):

- Calories 342
- Fat 33.3 g
- Carbohydrates 9.6 g
- Sugar 1.8 g
- Protein 7.8 g
- Cholesterol 0 mg

Cinnamon Apple Rice Pudding

Preparation Time: 10 minutes

Cooking Time: 15 minutes

Serve: 2

Ingredients:

- 1 cup of rice
- 1 tsp vanilla
- 1/4 apple, peeled and chopped
- 1/2 cup water
- 1 1/2 cup almond milk
- 1 tsp cinnamon
- 1 cinnamon stick

Directions:

1. Add all ingredients into the instant pot and stir well.
2. Seal pot with lid and cook on high for 15 minutes.
3. Once done, release pressure using quick release. Remove lid.
4. Stir and serve.

Nutritional Value (Amount per Serving):

- Calories 206
- Fat 11.5 g
- Carbohydrates 23.7 g
- Sugar 2.7 g
- Protein 3 g
- Cholesterol 0 mg

Conclusion

People who follow the Mediterranean Refresh Diet are known to have a longer life expectancy and are less likely to experience chronic diseases than others. But that doesn't mean giving up the pleasure of food, because the Mediterranean Diet is also about enjoying delicious food without neglecting your health.

This essential couple's cookbook has more than just tasty and wholesome Mediterranean Refresh recipes inside. You'll also find invaluable tips for streamlining your kitchen time, reducing food waste, and enhancing your meals with cooking hacks and simple techniques to add even more flavor to your favorite dishes.

Mediterranean Refresh Cooking for Two is your guide to quick-and-easy dishes sized right for a pair.

CPSIA information can be obtained
at www.ICGtesting.com
Printed in the USA
LVHW100851241021
701370LV00005B/332

9 781915 038913